the Storyteller's Workbook

AN INSPIRATIONAL, INTERACTIVE GUIDE TO THE CRAFT OF NOVEL WRITING

ADRIENNE YOUNG & ISABEL IBAÑEZ

A TarcherPerigee Book

tarcherperigee

an imprint of Penguin Random House LLC
penguinrandomhouse.com

Most TarcherPerigee books are available at special quantity discounts for bulk
purchase for sales promotions, premiums, fund-raising, and educational needs.
Special books or book excerpts also can be created to fit specific needs.
For details, write: SpecialMarkets@penguinrandomhouse.com.

Trade paperback ISBN: 9780593539439
Ebook ISBN: 9780593539446
Library of Congress Control Number: 2022934824

Printed in China
10 9 8 7 6 5 4 3 2 1

Book design by Isabel Ibañez

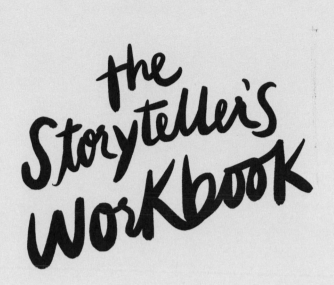

NAME: _____

_____

PROJECT: _____

_____

_____

CONTACT INFORMATION: _____

_____

_____

_____

WELCOME TO THE STORYTELLER'S WORKBOOK

We're glad you're here. But we have to start with a warning.

Setting out to write a novel is a daunting task, and there are so many voices out there telling you how to tame the ferocious beast that is your manuscript. As creatives, we've often struggled with formulas and guides that attempt to give us all the answers, and if that's what you are hoping to find in these pages, you'll be sorely disappointed.

But we have great news for you—you are the storyteller.

This workbook isn't an enchanted potion that will give you the ability to write your novel. Its intention is to help you access the storytelling superpower that has always lived within you.

We've made it as fluid and customizable as possible so that you create the rules, with questions along the way to spark your creativity and help you dig deep into the realm of your imagination. This is the story that only you can write, and *The Storyteller's Workbook* will keep you organized and focused while you work your magic.

Are you ready? We will tell you a secret: none of us ever are. But once you turn the page, we're in this together.

Ready, set, *go*.

TABLE OF CONTENTS
PART ONE: GETTING THE STORY DOWN

TABLE OF CONTENTS
PART TWO: GETTING THE STORY OUT THERE

PART ONE: GETTING THE STORY DOWN

CALENDAR

Daydreaming with headphones on while you stare out the window is where some of the best story development happens, but if you're going to ever hold that book in your hands, you need a game plan.

Start with the Bird's-Eye View on page 5 and label each box by month, no matter when you begin. Use this zoomed-out view to set your big intentions and envision your progress before you wade into the details. Once you have a vision for the work ahead, start breaking it down in the month-to-month calendar on page 6. Every writer works at a different pace, so you have plenty of flexibility to customize the calendar however you see fit. Setting goals can be stressful, so remember: this is a positive, creative space. Organize your goals by word count, chapters, or development milestones. It's completely up to you. Whether you decide to work by the week, the month, or to plan out your entire year, don't be afraid to tweak your plan along the way. Every book will have its own twists and turns.

Get out your sharpened pencil, your favorite gel pens, or the cute little stickers tucked into the back of the workbook.

It's time to get to work.

NOTES:

TO DO:

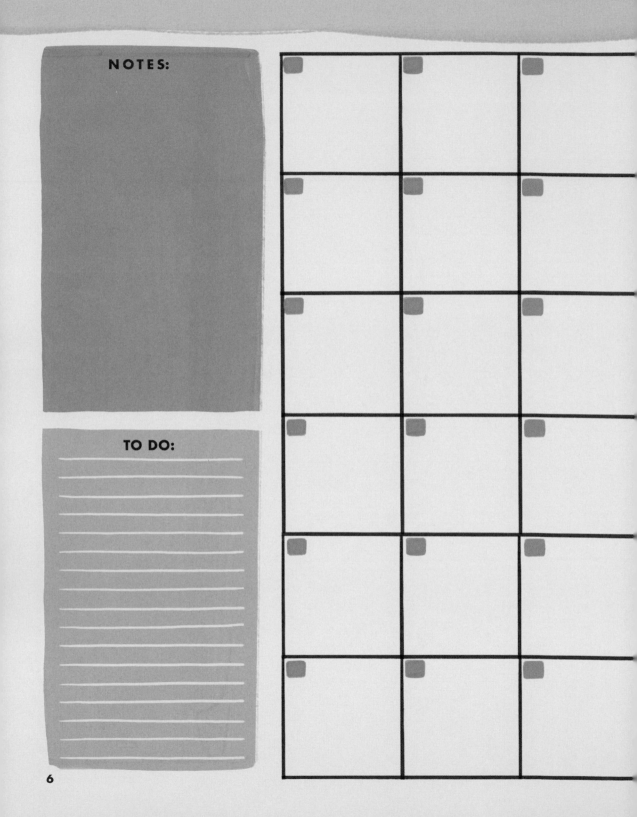

MONTH:

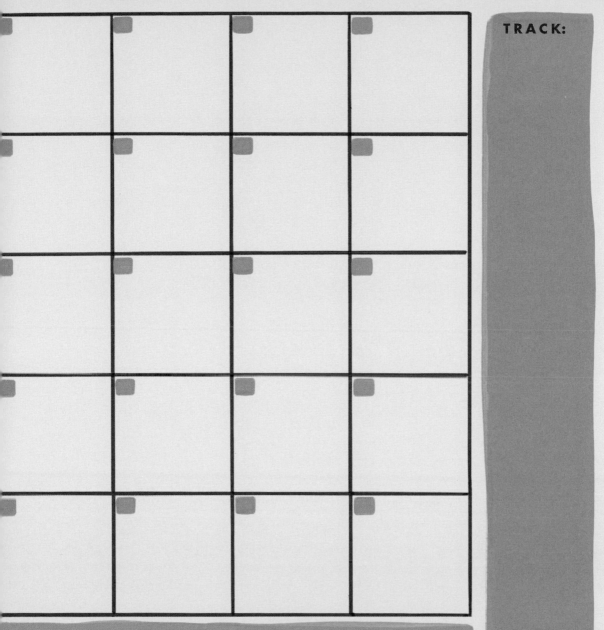

GOALS:

TO DO:

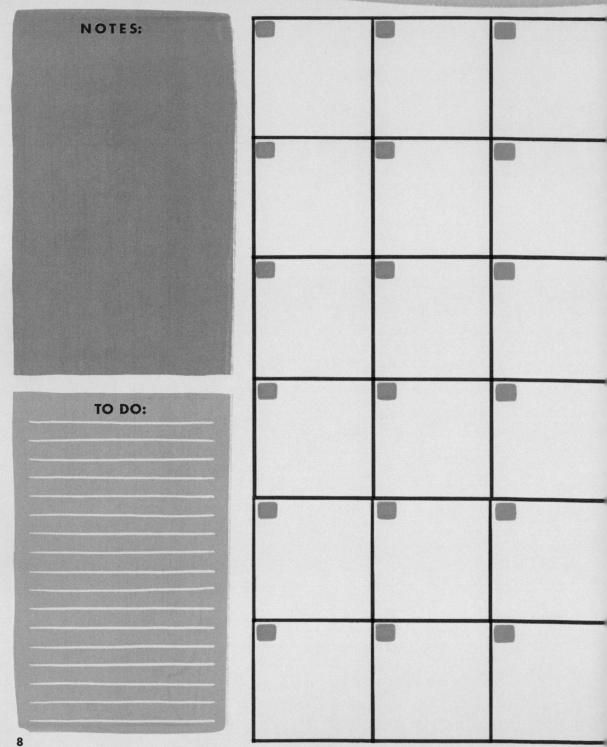

MONTH:

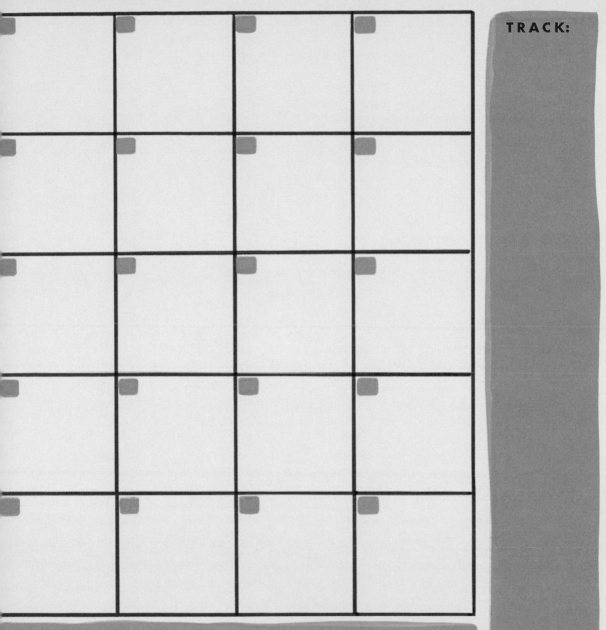

GOALS:

9

NOTES:

TO DO:

MONTH:

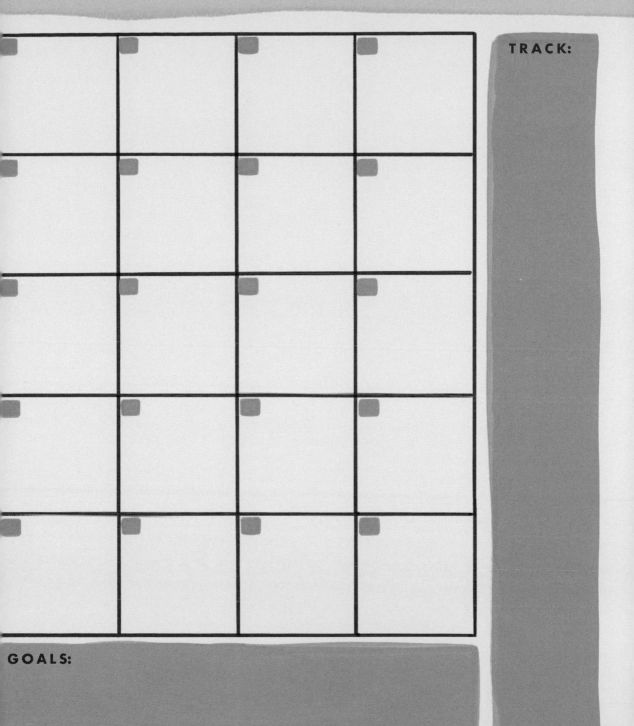

TRACK:

GOALS:

11

NOTES:

TO DO:

MONTH:

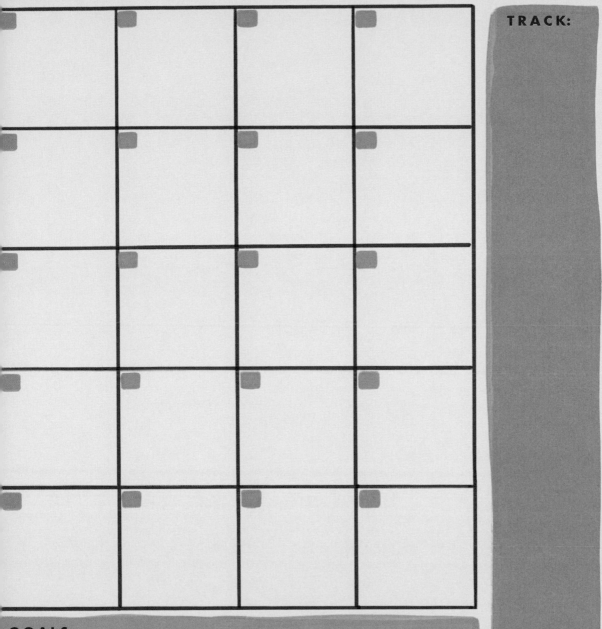

TRACK:

GOALS:

13

NOTES:

TO DO:

MONTH:

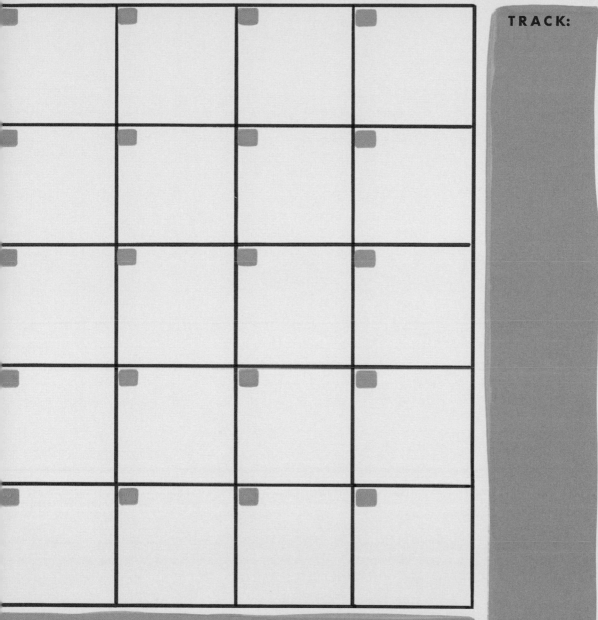

TRACK:

GOALS:

TO DO:

MONTH:

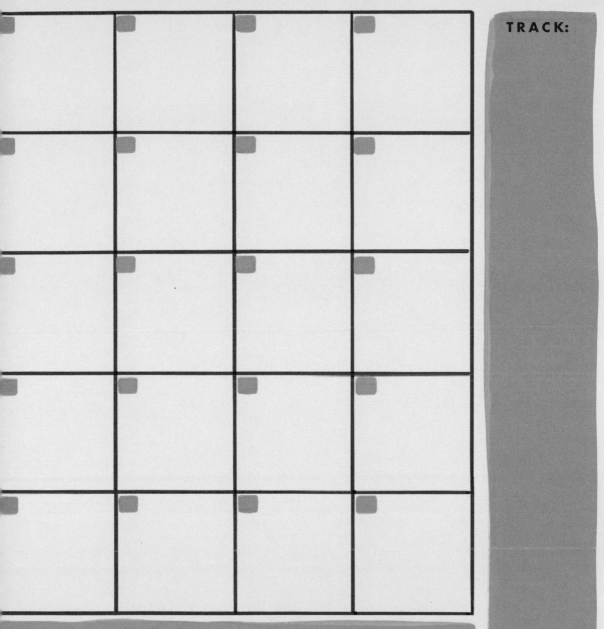

GOALS:

17

NOTES:

TO DO:

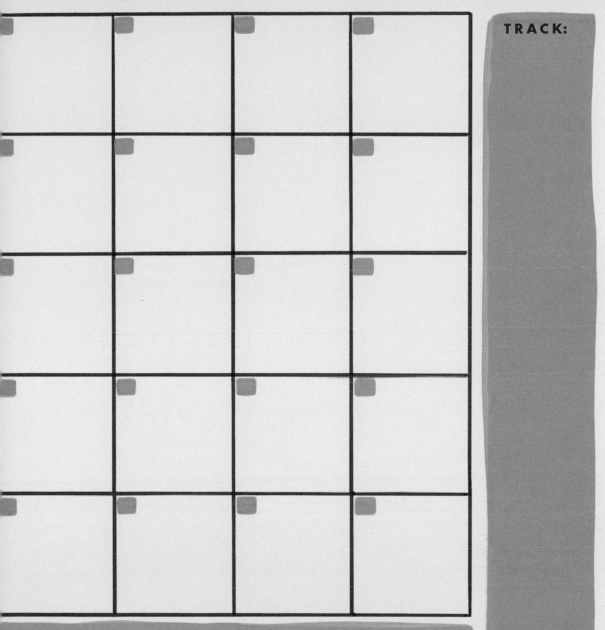

TRACK:

GOALS:

NOTES:

TO DO:

MONTH:

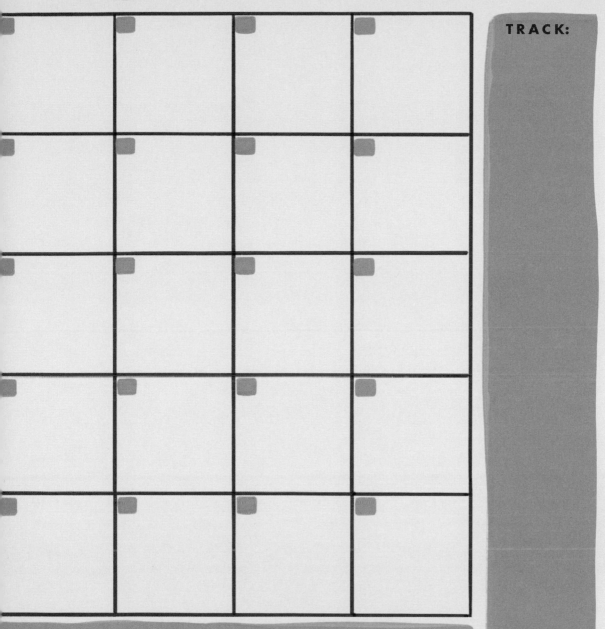

GOALS:

21

NOTES:

TO DO:

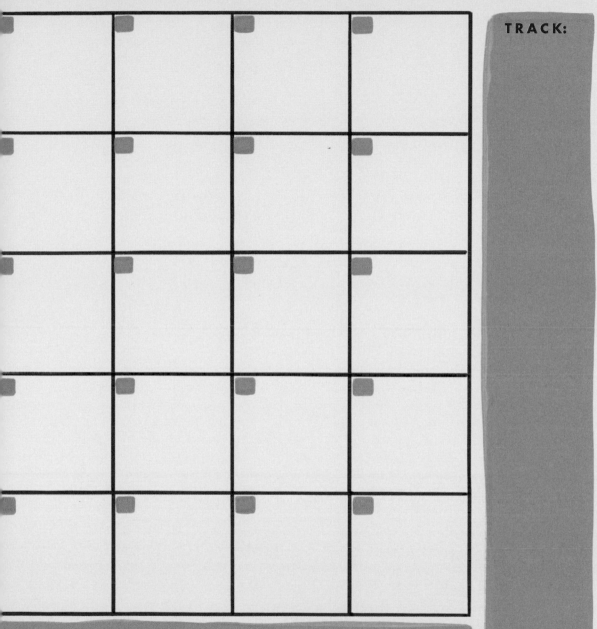

TRACK:

GOALS:

NOTES:

TO DO:

MONTH:

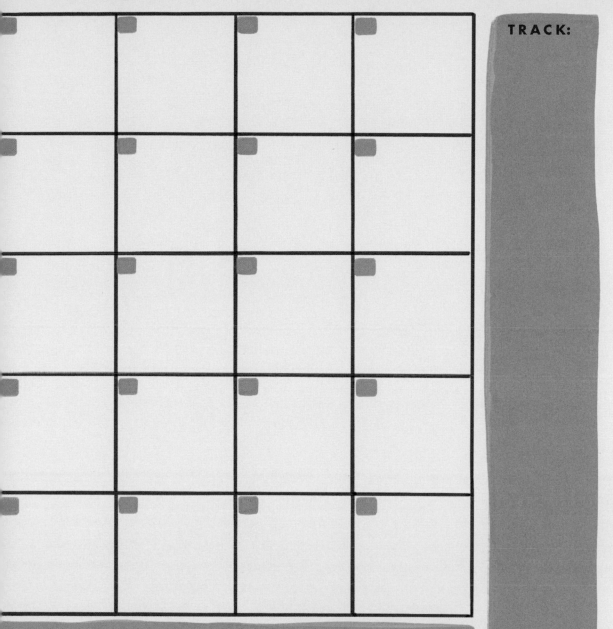

TRACK:

GOALS:

NOTES:

TO DO:

MONTH:

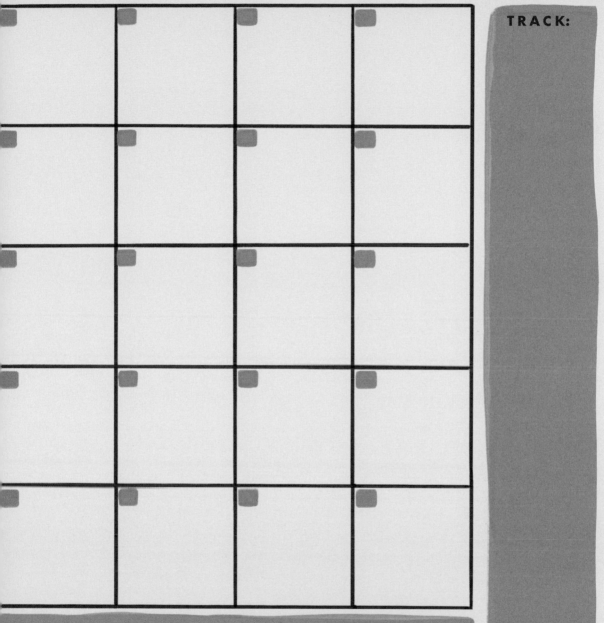

GOALS:

27

NOTES:

TO DO:

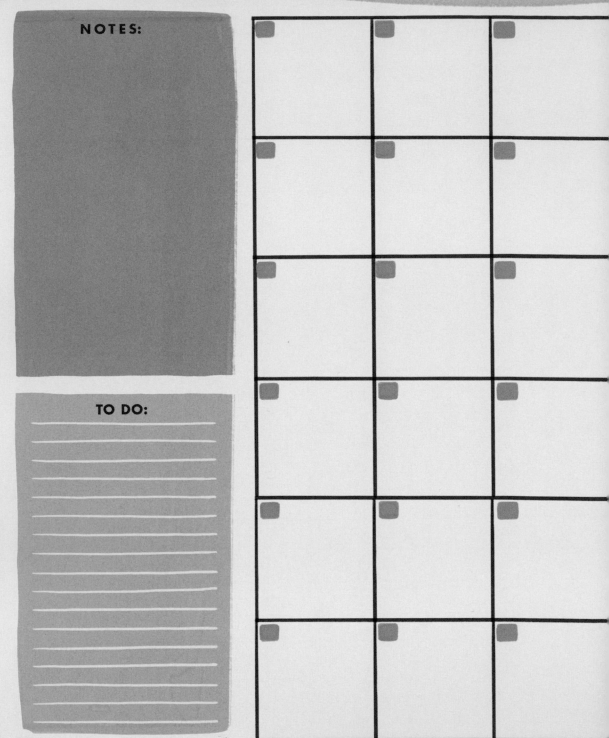

MONTH:

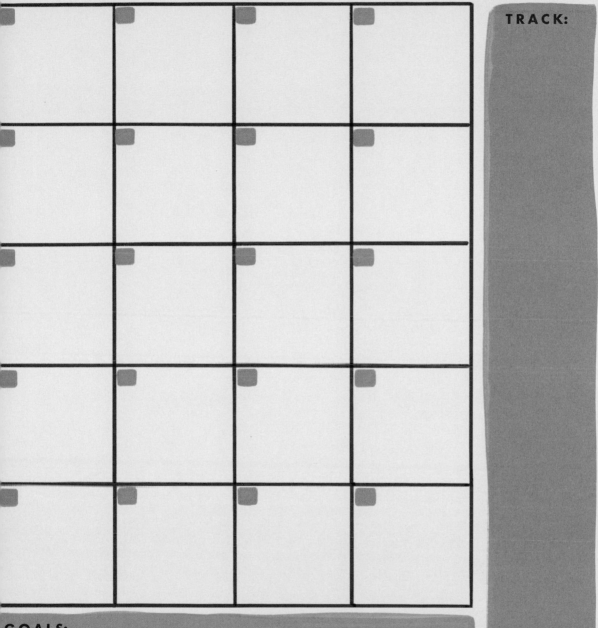

TRACK:

GOALS:

PRACTICE MAKES PROGRESS

Here's the deal: writing a book is hard. Really hard. It's easy to get overwhelmed by the work that lies ahead, and no matter how motivated you are at the outset, you're bound to hit some obstacles along the way. So, we're going to think of your book as a collection of forests, and each piece of that book as a tree.

Assign each forest in your Writer Woods any theme you like. For example, you could use hours spent working, chapters finished, or even word-count increments. Then give each tree a specific value—three hours of work, one chapter written, 1,000 words on the page. The end goal is the same: to color in each and every tree until you have reached your greater objective, whatever it may be.

Try to keep your goals realistic but still a bit challenging. This balance will be different for every writer, and it might take some trial and error. If you find that your plan isn't working for you, don't be afraid to change it up!

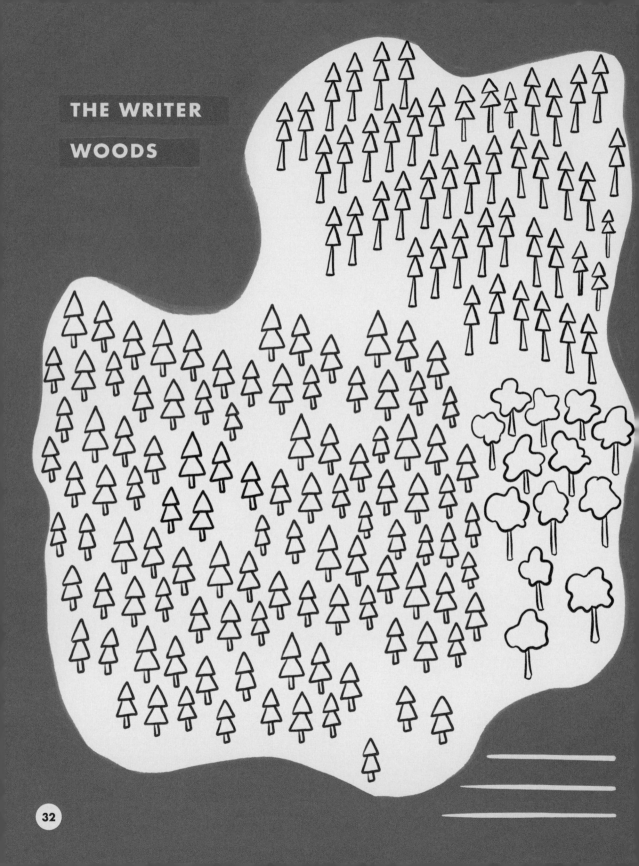

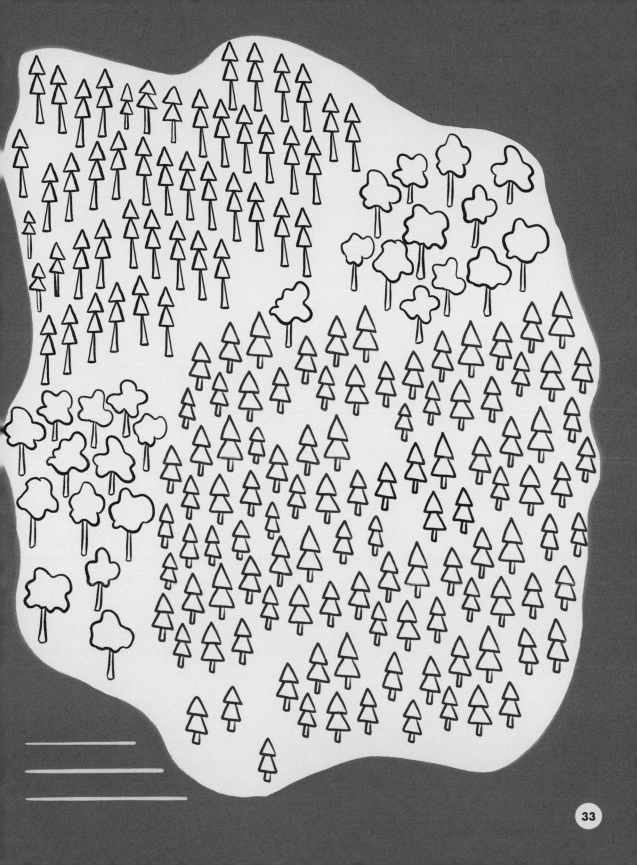

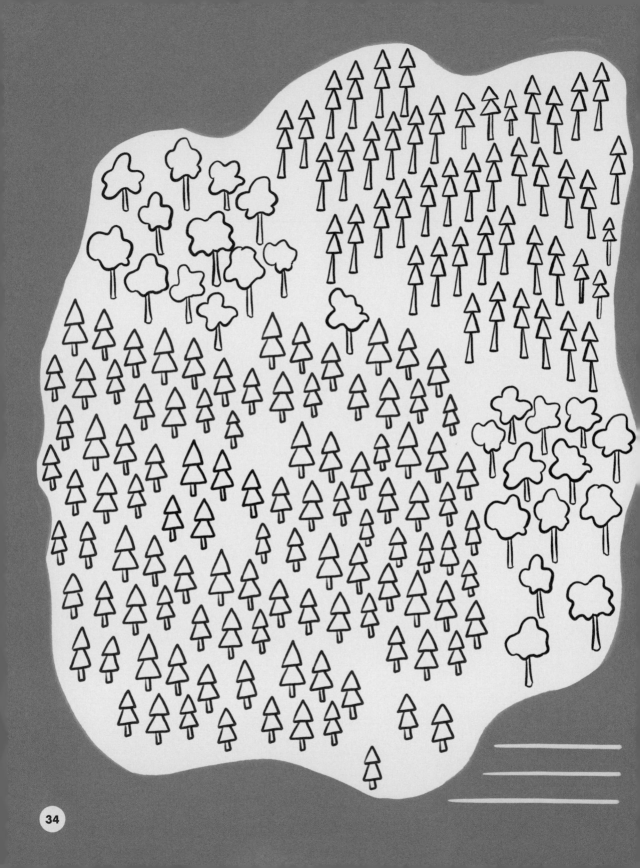

34

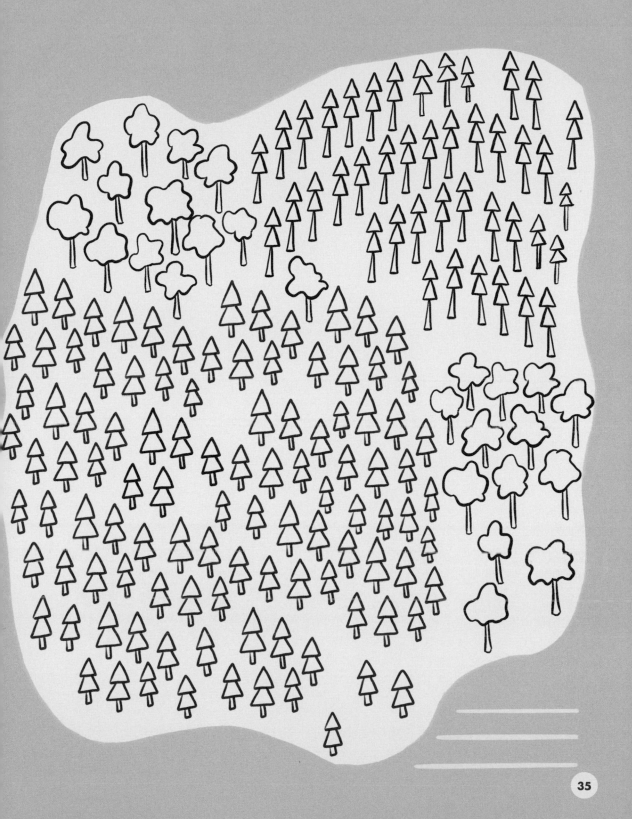

PLOTTERS & PANTSERS

Whether you're the no-nonsense writer who keeps a color-coded spreadsheet outline for your story (like Isabel) or the free-spirited discovery writer who likes to write where the wind blows you (like Adrienne), everyone needs a place to keep track of their story as it evolves. The longer the word count, the more of a beast a manuscript becomes. If you don't keep your perspective, it can—and will—devour you.

In the following pages, you'll find the wild, untamed space you need to create any kind of outline that works for you. Like to storyboard? Do it. Prefer a good old-fashioned bullet point setup? Do it. You can use any story structure system, with as much or as little detail as you like. Break it up by acts, story beats, scenes, chapters . . . whatever! If you love using note cards, we've included those as well (see pages 60–71) to help you visualize your scenes. You call all the shots here. Just take our advice and use a pencil with a working eraser. Story tends to have a mind of its own.

Need some inspiration?
Check out the examples on the next page.

WOVEN IN MOONLIGHT

I. CHAPTER ONE

A) introduce Ximena (decoy), Catalina (Condesa), the Keep and secondary characters. People are hungry. Ximena emotion: frustration and anger.

B) Catalina struggles to read the stars. Ximena weaves alone—See the magic in Inkasisa.

C) Atoc sends his messenger. (Glimpse of antagonist).

D) Hint of El Lobo, the vigilante. (Love interest ♡).

II. CHAPTER TWO

A) The message: a marriage proposal for Catalina

B) Introduce a hint of the priest. (antagonist #2)

C) Ximena learns Ana was Kidnapped, in a move to make them look weak. Ximena Kills the messenger.

III. CHAPTER THREE

A) Ximena and Catalina argue, and Ximena persuades Catalina to let her go to Atoc in her place.

B) Ximena learns the Estrella is missing.

C) Ximena and Sofia leave the Keep, they pass the drug fields.

D) Sofia is murdered.

the
Spinners

Tova wakes
to the call of
the Nightbird

Tova
Casts
the Runes

Clarity
magic &
set story
Into
motion

Intro
magic & myth

Jorrund calls
her to the
Ritual House

full circle
moment with
ending

Scene
one

World
& character
setup

Tova's
past

Establish
Backstory
& tension

Intro
world
conflict

Vigdis
lashes out
at Tova

Vigdis reports
village attack
to Bekah

Vigdis
as antagonist

tension
between
brothers

Jorrund's
role &
inner
conflict

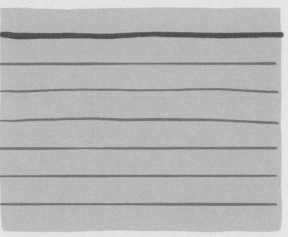

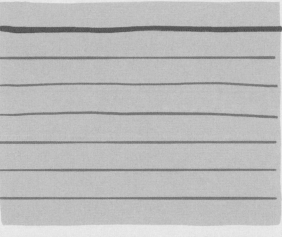

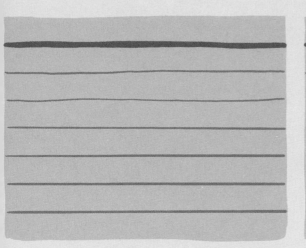

CHARACTER PROFILE GUIDES

We all know that character development can make or break a story, but how do you build characters that hook readers and compel them to keep turning the page? The answer: make them as realistic as possible. This doesn't mean that your character can't have a superpower or confront extraordinary circumstances. It means that when you boil that character down, you have what feels like a living, breathing human being that the reader can relate to, connect to, and care about.

The best way to achieve this is to get to know your characters on a deep level. You have to understand details about them, their lives, and their perspectives that the reader may never even discover, because those are the gems that drive their actions, reactions, and the little quirks that make them memorable.

This can only be accomplished by spending a lot of time with your protagonist, your antagonist, and even your supporting characters. Use these Character Profile Guides as a jumping-off point, but don't stop there. If there's a detail that captures your attention, explore it. Chances are, it's something your reader will latch on to.

If you're a writer who tends to discover your characters as you draft, fear not. You can use these guides at any part of your process. Come back and fill in the details as the character reveals them to you. This is your comprehensive reference to come back to again and again.

CHARACTER PROFILE GUIDE

NAME:

AGE: BIRTHDAY:

PHYSICAL APPEARANCE:

RELATION/CONNECTION TO MAIN CHARACTER:

EARLY LIFE:

ROLE/OCCUPATION IN THE STORY: *Who are they? Why are they here?*

SPIRITUAL/IDEOLOGICAL/PHILOSOPHICAL BELIEFS:

THE LIE THEY BELIEVE:

WHAT THEY WANT MOST IN THE WORLD:

WHAT THEY NEED *(whether they know it or not)*:

MOTIVATION: *What drives their actions and opinions?*

GHOSTS: *Greatest fear? What haunts them?*

FLIGHT, FIGHT, FREEZE: *When tragedy strikes, what do they do?*

PERSONALITY TYPE (*Myers-Briggs, enneagram, etc.*):

FAVORITE MEMORY? MOST PAINFUL MEMORY?

_____
_____
_____
_____
_____
_____
_____
_____
_____
_____
_____
_____
_____
_____
_____
_____

SECRETS:

STRENGTHS:

WEAKNESSES:

MORAL CODE: *What are the rules they live by? What line will they not cross?*

_____
_____
_____
_____
_____

CHARACTER ARC: *Overall evolution of the individual character and their growth or decline.*

_____
_____
_____
_____
_____
_____
_____
_____
_____
_____
_____
_____
_____
_____

CHARACTER PROFILE GUIDE

NAME:

AGE: **BIRTHDAY:**

PHYSICAL APPEARANCE:

RELATION/CONNECTION TO MAIN CHARACTER:

EARLY LIFE:

_____
_____
_____
_____
_____
_____
_____
_____
_____
_____
_____
_____
_____

ROLE/OCCUPATION IN THE STORY: *Who are they? Why are they here?*

SPIRITUAL/IDEOLOGICAL/PHILOSOPHICAL BELIEFS:

THE LIE THEY BELIEVE:

WHAT THEY WANT MOST IN THE WORLD:

WHAT THEY NEED *(whether they know it or not)*:

MOTIVATION: *What drives their actions and opinions?*

GHOSTS: *Greatest fear? What haunts them?*

FLIGHT, FIGHT, FREEZE: *When tragedy strikes, what do they do?*

PERSONALITY TYPE (*Myers-Briggs, enneagram, etc.*):

FAVORITE MEMORY? MOST PAINFUL MEMORY?

_____
_____
_____
_____
_____
_____
_____
_____
_____
_____
_____
_____
_____
_____
_____

SECRETS:

STRENGTHS:

WEAKNESSES:

MORAL CODE: *What are the rules they live by? What line will they not cross?*

_____

_____

_____

_____

_____

CHARACTER ARC: *Overall evolution of the individual character and their growth or decline.*

_____

_____

_____

_____

_____

_____

_____

_____

_____

_____

_____

_____

_____

CHARACTER PROFILE GUIDE

NAME:

AGE: BIRTHDAY:

PHYSICAL APPEARANCE:

RELATION/CONNECTION TO MAIN CHARACTER:

EARLY LIFE:

_____
_____
_____
_____
_____
_____
_____
_____
_____
_____
_____
_____
_____
_____

ROLE/OCCUPATION IN THE STORY: *Who are they? Why are they here?*

SPIRITUAL/IDEOLOGICAL/PHILOSOPHICAL BELIEFS:

THE LIE THEY BELIEVE:

WHAT THEY WANT MOST IN THE WORLD:

WHAT THEY NEED *(whether they know it or not)*:

MOTIVATION: *What drives their actions and opinions?*

GHOSTS: *Greatest fear? What haunts them?*

FLIGHT, FIGHT, FREEZE: *When tragedy strikes, what do they do?*

PERSONALITY TYPE (*Myers-Briggs, enneagram, etc.*):

FAVORITE MEMORY? MOST PAINFUL MEMORY?

_____
_____
_____
_____
_____
_____
_____
_____
_____
_____
_____
_____
_____
_____
_____

SECRETS:

STRENGTHS:

WEAKNESSES:

MORAL CODE: *What are the rules they live by? What line will they not cross?*

_____
_____
_____
_____
_____

CHARACTER ARC: *Overall evolution of the individual character and their growth or decline.*

_____
_____
_____
_____
_____
_____
_____
_____
_____
_____
_____
_____
_____
_____

CHARACTER PROFILE GUIDE

NAME:

AGE: BIRTHDAY:

PHYSICAL APPEARANCE:

RELATION/CONNECTION TO MAIN CHARACTER:

EARLY LIFE:

_____
_____
_____
_____
_____
_____
_____
_____
_____
_____
_____
_____
_____

ROLE/OCCUPATION IN THE STORY: *Who are they? Why are they here?*

SPIRITUAL/IDEOLOGICAL/PHILOSOPHICAL BELIEFS:

THE LIE THEY BELIEVE:

WHAT THEY WANT MOST IN THE WORLD:

_____
_____
_____
_____

WHAT THEY NEED *(whether they know it or not)*:

_____
_____
_____
_____

MOTIVATION: *What drives their actions and opinions?*

GHOSTS: *Greatest fear? What haunts them?*

FLIGHT, FIGHT, FREEZE: *When tragedy strikes, what do they do?*

PERSONALITY TYPE (*Myers-Briggs, enneagram, etc.*): _____
_____
_____
_____

FAVORITE MEMORY? MOST PAINFUL MEMORY?

_____

_____

_____

_____

_____

_____

_____

_____

_____

_____

_____

_____

_____

_____

_____

_____

SECRETS:

STRENGTHS:

WEAKNESSES:

MORAL CODE: *What are the rules they live by? What line will they not cross?*

_____

_____

_____

_____

_____

CHARACTER ARC: *Overall evolution of the individual character and their growth or decline.*

_____

_____

_____

_____

_____

_____

_____

_____

_____

_____

_____

_____

CHARACTER PROFILE GUIDE

NAME:

AGE: BIRTHDAY:

PHYSICAL APPEARANCE:

RELATION/CONNECTION TO MAIN CHARACTER:

EARLY LIFE:

_____
_____
_____
_____
_____
_____
_____
_____
_____
_____
_____
_____
_____

ROLE/OCCUPATION IN THE STORY: *Who are they? Why are they here?*

SPIRITUAL/IDEOLOGICAL/PHILOSOPHICAL BELIEFS:

THE LIE THEY BELIEVE:

WHAT THEY WANT MOST IN THE WORLD:

WHAT THEY NEED *(whether they know it or not)*:

MOTIVATION: *What drives their actions and opinions?*

GHOSTS: *Greatest fear? What haunts them?*

FLIGHT, FIGHT, FREEZE: *When tragedy strikes, what do they do?*

PERSONALITY TYPE (*Myers-Briggs, enneagram, etc.*):

FAVORITE MEMORY? MOST PAINFUL MEMORY?

_____
_____
_____
_____
_____
_____
_____
_____
_____
_____
_____
_____
_____
_____

SECRETS:

STRENGTHS:

WEAKNESSES:

MORAL CODE: *What are the rules they live by? What line will they not cross?*

_____
_____
_____
_____
_____

CHARACTER ARC: *Overall evolution of the individual character and their growth or decline.*

_____
_____
_____
_____
_____
_____
_____
_____
_____
_____
_____
_____
_____
_____
_____

CHARACTER PROFILE GUIDE

NAME:

AGE: BIRTHDAY:

PHYSICAL APPEARANCE:

RELATION/CONNECTION TO MAIN CHARACTER:

EARLY LIFE:

_____
_____
_____
_____
_____
_____
_____
_____
_____
_____
_____
_____
_____
_____

ROLE/OCCUPATION IN THE STORY: *Who are they? Why are they here?*

SPIRITUAL/IDEOLOGICAL/PHILOSOPHICAL BELIEFS:

THE LIE THEY BELIEVE:

WHAT THEY WANT MOST IN THE WORLD:

WHAT THEY NEED *(whether they know it or not)*:

MOTIVATION: *What drives their actions and opinions?*

GHOSTS: *Greatest fear? What haunts them?*

FLIGHT, FIGHT, FREEZE: *When tragedy strikes, what do they do?*

PERSONALITY TYPE (*Myers-Briggs, enneagram, etc.*):

FAVORITE MEMORY? MOST PAINFUL MEMORY?

_____
_____
_____
_____
_____
_____
_____
_____
_____
_____
_____
_____
_____
_____
_____
_____

SECRETS:

STRENGTHS:

WEAKNESSES:

MORAL CODE: *What are the rules they live by? What line will they not cross?*

_____

_____

_____

_____

_____

CHARACTER ARC: *Overall evolution of the individual character and their growth or decline.*

_____

_____

_____

_____

_____

_____

_____

_____

_____

_____

_____

_____

_____

_____

Whether your story takes place in a medieval fantasy kingdom, a planet in a distant solar system, or a remote mountain range of the Pacific Northwest where a modern-day cult has set up a settlement, one thing will always be true: you have to build your world as meticulously as you build your characters.

Having a thorough understanding of your world and how it works will manifest in the tiniest of details that come to the surface on the page. The reader will likely never read a book about the fictional world you've created, but as its creator, you should be able to write one.

The following guide will take you through the ground level of world building so that you can begin to explore your world and how it works. If you don't know the nitty-gritty before you start drafting, that's okay. Revisit it as you gain clarity and start asking questions, even when you don't have the answers yet.

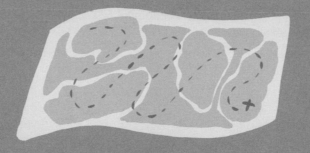

WORLD-BUILDING GUIDE

WORLD NAME:

LANDSCAPE *(landforms, bodies of water, atmosphere, types of terrain—coastal/mountain/desert):*

CLIMATE & SEASONS:

SURROUNDING WORLD *(nearby cities, countries, kingdoms, planets):*

_____

_____

_____

_____

_____

_____

_____

_____

NOTABLE LANDMARKS
(cities, rivers, cafes, streets, castles, alleys, crofts, houses):

LIFE-FORMS *(human, mythological, supernatural, robot, alien)*:

SUPERNATURAL ELEMENTS & MAGIC SYSTEMS:

_____
_____
_____
_____
_____
_____
_____
_____
_____
_____

SOCIETY STRUCTURE *(tribal, democratic, monarchical, run by a council or eldership)*:

RULER: *Who rules this world and what kind of ruler are they?*

WORLD HISTORY: *What in the past made this world what it is today? Think both macro and micro.*

GREATEST THREAT:

TECHNOLOGY *(primitive, advanced, writer-created):*

WEAPONS:

RESOURCES: *What can be found in the world that is used for profit, survival, or trade?*

_____

_____

_____

_____

_____

_____

_____

_____

_____

_____

_____

_____

_____

_____

_____

_____

BUILDING MATERIALS: *What do people use to build structures in this world? Brick, stone, steel, natural materials?*

CLOTHING, FOOTWEAR & JEWELRY:

TRANSPORTATION: *How do people travel short and long distances?*

FOOD:

_____   _____
_____   _____
_____   _____
_____   _____
_____   _____
_____   _____
_____   _____

ECONOMICS: *What fuels the economy of this world? What is the currency? What do people do to make a living?*

PLANTS & ANIMALS:

_____   _____
_____   _____
_____   _____
_____   _____
_____   _____
_____   _____
_____   _____

SPIRITUAL BELIEFS & SYSTEMS:

Speculative fiction writers aren't the only storytellers who may find a map useful in the writing process. It's helpful to have a visual guide that highlights all of the most important places in your book. Whether you're writing contemporary, fantasy, sci-fi, or historical fiction, your novel takes place somewhere, and a map is your reference point for keeping all the facts straight.

Contrary to what you might think, you don't have to be an artist to create a map. You also don't need a finished book. Sketching out the world while you're still in the weeds of drafting might even help you discover things about the story that you didn't know were there. Not sure where to start? That's okay.

On the following pages you'll find a handy checklist with some things to consider before you put pencil to paper.

Mapmaking Checklist

☐ Make a list of meaningful places in your world. Does your climactic moment happen in a bake shop? At the edge of a cliff? Do your characters make camp at a specific lake? Be sure to include these places, along with any relevant physical and natural landmarks.

☐ Next, draw the border of your world. This doesn't have to be perfect, but you do want to think about where the bulk of your tale takes place. Ask yourself questions as you go along. Does your kingdom or town have a coastline? If so, does it have an impact on your story? Asking these questions helps you home in on where the focal point of your map will be. It may also be a good idea to think about the other countries or territories surrounding your setting, as well as traveling distance to them.

☐ Now it's time to figure out the particular landscape of your world. This can always change, but it's useful to work through the environment of your story. Are there grasslands? Tundra? Or is there a desert encroaching on your character's home? Also, remember that water flows downhill toward a larger body of water, eventually meandering into the ocean. If you'd like to draw every tree, by all means go for it, but simply writing where and what everything is will suffice.

■ Drop in all points of interest and don't sweat getting the drawing exactly right. Even basic circles are fine to denote cities, and squiggles for lakes or rivers. The goal is to show where everything is.

■ Label every landmark. We can't tell you how often the name of an established street or mountain range has evaded us while we're tinkering in a scene. The same city might be called three different things by the time you're through the draft. But with every landmark properly named, your map will help you stay consistent while drafting.

■ Last, show roads or streets your characters often travel in order to keep track of their journeys and how long it might take to get from one place to another.

Use the next several pages to start dreaming up your world and remember that your map will evolve as your story does. Come back to it throughout your writing process to make as many updates and changes as you like.

SKETCHING PAGES

Sometimes you just need a visual. Maps, blueprints, diagrams, family trees . . . the sky is the limit. This is your space to explore and create.

BRAINSTORMING PAGES

Tinker, conceptualize, or play to your heart's content. Use the following pages to record research, freewrite, or even break down a scene if needed. Don't be afraid to get lost in the what if.

PART TWO:

GETTING THE STORY OUT THERE

REVISION CHECKLIST

Completing the first draft is arguably the most daunting aspect of writing a book. But typing THE END doesn't mean the work is done. Revision is where a lot of the magic happens in storytelling, and though it's a lot of work, it's also a lot of fun when you begin to see all those words and pages start to look like the novel you first envisioned.

Keep a running to-do list as you write so that it's waiting when you are ready to tackle your revisions. Things you might jot down could include character or story line changes, geographical edits, tweaks on pacing, or feedback from critique partners or beta readers. If you're new to either of these terms, don't worry—they're just fancy labels.

Critique Partner (*n.*) A critique partner is a fellow writer who has agreed to read and critique your work in order to help you make it stronger. This might include notes relating to plot, character, or style.

Beta Reader (*n.*) A beta reader is a kind of test reader, who gives you feedback based on their reading experience. This feedback will typically focus on things like plot holes, pacing, or identifying the elements of the story that readers might most respond to and resonate with.

As you revise, it's also a good idea to direct your attention to elements you are overusing. If you see words, phrases, or descriptions that are popping up frequently in the draft, you can save yourself some time by writing them down in your Polishing Checklist (page 149) so that you can search for them later.

In order to build out an effective, organized plan for this stage, we like to think of revisions in three categories that indicate both their impact on the story and the amount of work they require to execute:

Big, or macro, revisions will be at the top of this list, with tasks like structural changes or redrafting an act of the book.

Medium- or intermediate-level revisions are things like adjustments to the protagonist's motivations or the continuity of a particular theme.

The last category is your small, or micro, revisions. These are little changes, like tweaking a description, changing the name of something throughout the document, or tightening dialogue as you go.

Divvy up your revision checklist in whatever way feels best to you, keeping in mind that you can always shift your approach.

POLISHING CHECKLIST

If you've finished revising, it's time to polish, polish, polish! The manuscript is finished, even if it feels like the story will never be "done." You have a hefty word count and a book you love, but before it can be read by publishing professionals, you have to go in with a fine-tooth comb and find any snags that are still lurking.

SPELL-CHECK

It's a good idea to run a thorough spell-check on the entire manuscript, even if your program corrects you automatically as you type. If you have words you've created in your story that can't be found in a dictionary or encyclopedia, be sure to keep a running list of these terms so you can check your consistency with spelling.

GRAMMAR CHECK

If you're pretty good with grammar, running a standard check through a word processing program might be enough. If you don't consider yourself particularly skilled, you might consider enlisting a professional, such as a freelance copyeditor, or a writer friend with a good eye to give the manuscript a look.

FORMATTING

There are industry standards when it comes to formatting, especially when submitting a manuscript to an agent or editor. These standards ensure that the work is easy to read and mark up, if needed.

- Convert your manuscript to a Microsoft Word doc if you've drafted it in another program.
- Margins on all sides should be set to 1 inch.
- Use 12-point Times New Roman font.
- Use double spacing on the entire document.
- Insert page numbers beginning on the first page of Chapter One.
- Be sure each chapter has a distinct chapter heading, whether you're using numbers or specific titles.

TITLE PAGE

Include the title in all caps and your name at the center of the first page. Your contact information should be in the bottom left-hand corner.

FIRST AND LAST LINES

Revisit the first and last lines of every single chapter. Make sure your opening lines pull the reader in and provide a sense of immediacy. Your last lines should make sure the reader turns that page.

PASSIVE LANGUAGE

In your final reads, pay special attention to passive language and extraneous word usage that bogs a scene down.

REPETITION

Use the space opposite as you draft and revise to identify elements you might be overusing. These might be words, phrases, backstory tidbits, or even exclamation marks. When you're ready to polish, use the word search function to tackle them one at a time.

Few writers are lucky enough to start a project with a great title that sees the story through to the end. For most of us, we're writing under a working title that we know is temporary, and once publishers get involved, it can change more than once. Keep this in mind before you get too emotionally attached to a title. Literary agents, book editors, and marketing and sales teams will all weigh in at some point, so while you should be intentional in developing a title, you should also hold it with an open hand.

That said, you still need a title for your book, and finding the right one isn't as simple as making it sound nice. A title has a job to do. The story that exists inside the pages of a book is the most important part of the package, but it's still just a part. It will be concealed from readers behind a cover and . . . a title. This is all part of a book's packaging. The cover's job is to get the reader's eyes to stop when they are scanning a shelf and, you hope, pick up the book.

The title's job is to:

■ Intrigue the reader. Inviting the reader into the actual story through the title can be hit or miss. Anything too literal or on the nose can backfire. Imagine picking up a novel titled *Zombie Story*. Not too interesting, right? But when you find that satisfying balance between fact and mystery, it can reel a reader in. We could reimagine the title as something like *Tale of the Undead*.

■ Convey a sense of the writing or mood. Wordy, poetic titles might be a good fit if you're a lyrical writer and you want the voice of the book to come through. Or you might focus on setting a clear tone, with something bright and punchy for a rom-com or something dark and ominous for a thriller.

■ Get the reader to ask a question. Sometimes the best titles are ones that simply make the reader curious. This can be a play on words, a seemingly paradoxical phrase, or something that at first glance doesn't make sense. The key here is to make sure that the title is still anchored in the story somehow, even if the reader doesn't put it together until after they've read the book. Using our zombie example above, what if the book was called *Dinner with the Undead*? This immediately gives a reader an image in their mind. Maybe even a shocking one, since we know that zombies eat people. From there, the imagination does the rest.

The greatest feat is getting a title to fulfill all three of these jobs, and that isn't an easy thing to do. For some books, it's impossible. The thing to remember is that getting even one of these elements right is enough to give you a title that does your story justice. Not only will you have a good chance of the reader opening the cover or turning over the book to read the description—you might even get them to glance at the first page.

The purpose of this exercise is to help you narrow down what you want from your title and develop some options until you run across the one that you not only love but that is also capable of doing the job you need it to do.

TITLE WORKSHEET

In the space below, jot down some recent titles that have caught your eye. They don't necessarily have to be in the same category or genre as your story. Can't think of many? Visit your local bookstore and peruse the section that you think your book would be shelved in.

_____   _____

_____   _____

_____   _____

_____   _____

_____   _____

_____   _____

_____   _____

Now, shift your focus to your story. What elements make it special? What sets it apart from other books in the genre? What do you think readers will connect most with?

_____

_____

_____

_____

_____

_____

_____

_____

Think of as many adjectives as you can that describe the mood, tone, or feel of your story. If it was a song, how would it be described? Upbeat? Haunting? Humorous? Write down every adjective that pops into your head.

_____ _____ _____

_____ _____ _____

_____ _____ _____

_____ _____ _____

_____ _____ _____

_____ _____ _____

_____ _____ _____

_____ _____ _____

Now, identify nouns with significance in your story—people, places, or things that are specific to your book and that play key roles. Think outside the box here.

_____ _____ _____ _____

_____ _____ _____ _____

_____ _____ _____ _____

_____ _____ _____ _____

_____ _____ _____ _____

_____ _____ _____ _____

_____ _____ _____ _____

_____ _____ _____ _____

Identify words in your book that are unique to its world. These could include the name of a fictional race, a term for a magic system, or even an object that is central to the story line.

_____ _____ _____ _____

_____ _____ _____ _____

_____ _____ _____ _____

_____ _____ _____ _____

_____ _____ _____ _____

_____ _____ _____ _____

_____ _____ _____ _____

_____ _____ _____ _____

Are there any particularly catchy or provocative lines from the manuscript that could work as a title?

_____

_____

_____

_____

_____

_____

_____

_____

_____

_____

What are the main themes present in the story?

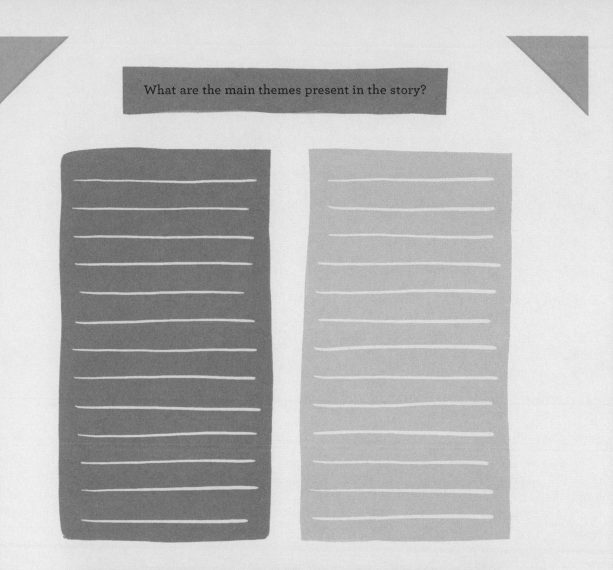

What emotion do you want to evoke in the reader through your title? How do you want them to feel?

POSSIBLE TITLES

Use this page as a catchall for any title or combination of words that come up while you're working. Remember, even bad ideas are welcome here. Sometimes they shake loose the good ones.

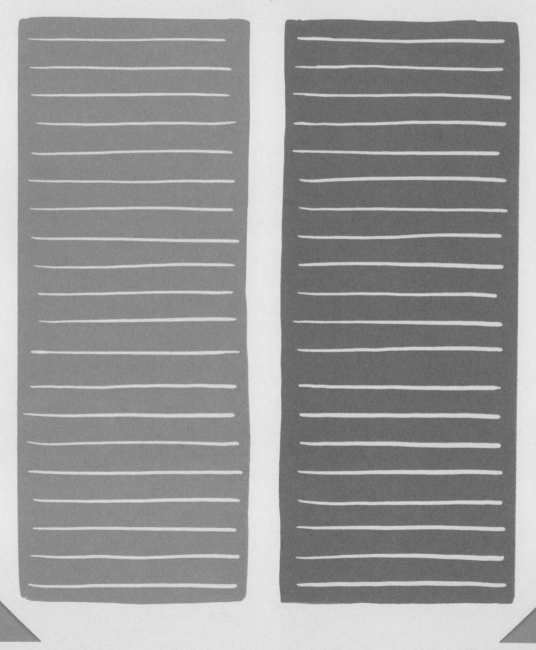

THE PITCH

Every writer will have to craft a pitch at some point, but how exactly do you do it? First, it's helpful for you to understand exactly what a pitch is and what it's used for. A pitch is a concise description that greatly condenses the breadth of the story while also retaining its most compelling aspects. Its purpose is to give the writer a straightforward way to communicate about the book to agents, editors, or other industry professionals while also catching their attention. There are both short and long forms, but no matter the length, every pitch will contain the same crucial components.

Simmering an entire novel down to just a few sentences isn't an easy task, and you should prepare yourself now to sacrifice some of your favorite details in the process. There's no way to fit everything you want someone to know about the book into the pitch, so we are going to zero in on the must-haves.

On the following pages, you'll find a short pitch for Adrienne's *Sky in the Deep* and a long pitch for Isabel's *Written in Starlight* to help you visualize how these elements work together to deliver a big impact.

The worksheet that follows will help you identify the key essentials of your story: the hook, the who, the central conflict, the goal, and the stakes.

→ WHO!

(Eelyn) has been raised as a warrior to fight in a generations-old blood feud between two clans, but her life is forever changed the day she sees the impossible on the battlefield—her brother, fighting alongside the enemy.

The brother she watched die five years ago.

↳ HOOK!

GOaL! ↑

When she's taken prisoner and forced to live among his new family, Eelyn must face her brother's betrayal and discover what really happened the day she lost him before the enemies that surround her can take her life and her honor.

↓ central conflict!

↓ Stakes!

→ Hook!

→ WHO?

Catalina Quiroga, countess of Inkasisa, has lost everything. The throne, her home, her best friend. Banished to the Yanu Jungle by the new queen of Inkasisa, Catalina will have to use all of her wits to survive the predators lurking beneath the vivid green canopy.

But when she stumbles across Manuel, the son of her former general and the boy she loved as a young girl, she manages to convince him to find Paititi, the lost city of gold, home to the Illari tribe hidden in the jungle depths. With their help, she might have a chance of reclaiming her birthright.

↑ Central Conflict!

Together they'll face mythical beasts, treacherous earth magic, and lethal traps to find Paititi. If they survive the search, Catalina will propose marriage to the Illari King, securing an alliance against her enemies in Inkasisa, but she'll have to set aside her growing feelings for Manuel in order for her desperate plan to work.

↰ GOAL

Goal #2 ↰

Meanwhile the Illari face a dangerous opposition of their own and before they can agree to becoming allies, Catalina will have to prove herself and earn their trust by eliminating Umaq, a priest whose god-given blood magic threatens the jungle lands and everything the Illari hold dear. If Catalina fails, she'll never be able to go home and fulfill her destiny as the rightful queen of Inkasisa.

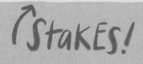 Stakes!

PITCH WORKSHEET

What is the hook? This is the opening element of the story that gets
the reader invested and compels them to turn the page.

_____

_____

_____

_____

_____

Who is the story about? What is the most essential information about
your main character that you must convey?

_____

_____

_____

_____

_____

What is the central conflict? Your story likely has multiple conflicts
and points of tension, but identify the most meaningful one—
the conflict your story hinges on.

_____

_____

_____

_____

What is the goal? What must the protagonist do to solve the central conflict?

_____

_____

_____

_____

_____

_____

_____

_____

_____

What are the stakes? What will happen if your protagonist does not succeed in reaching their goal?

_____

_____

_____

_____

_____

_____

_____

_____

_____

Now, revisit your answers to each question and trim them down, eliminating unnecessary words or repetitive information. The pitch should be snappy, with as little meandering as possible. See if you can put the elements together in a just a few sentences, beginning with the hook and ending with the stakes. It might take a few tries, so be patient with yourself.

THE SYNOPSIS

Similar to a pitch, your synopsis is a summary. But where the pitch sacrifices significant details for the sake of brevity, the synopsis lets you dig into the meat of the book to give a more thorough look at the wider story. It also answers all the questions that the pitch might pose, along with giving away the ending.

If you're planning to query literary agents, you'll need to have a synopsis on hand. Many agents will require that you submit a synopsis in your query package, or they may request one to learn more about the story if you've piqued their interest. It will also come in handy after you've signed with an agent, as they will need it to shop your book to publishers.

Writing a synopsis can feel really overwhelming, and there is more than one type of synopsis that can be used for different purposes. Be sure to read the guidelines, which should include a page or word count and given by agents or whomever you're writing the synopsis for before finalizing. This information can usually be found on their website. One thing synopses all have in common: they take the reader through the story step by step.

This is where your outline will come in handy. Even if you're not a plotter, you should have developed some sort of organized outline through the drafting and revision process that gives you the panoramic perspective of your book as a whole. It's useful to refer to this outline when you're crafting a synopsis, because you will essentially be using your story structure as a road map, beat for beat. On page 169, you'll find Adrienne's synopsis of *Fable* so you can see these elements in action.

Some tips to keep in mind as you move through the worksheet:

Keep it focused. Similar to the pitch, there is no way to include every detail about the story that you find interesting or special. Be sure that every element introduced in your synopsis has earned its place there and is completely necessary.

Get to the point. Resist the urge to go down rabbit holes or to overexplain.

Watch for repetition. If you've provided information in one part of the synopsis through character or world introduction, be sure not to restate it later in another part of the synopsis. Every word counts.

Only introduce characters and story lines that are absolutely crucial to either the central conflict of the story or the protagonist's internal character arc.

Use your voice. Be sure that the rote of going story beat to story beat doesn't erase your voice as a writer. This isn't the place to show off all your skills, but the synopsis should have at least a hint of your writing style.

Make sure your stakes are clear. The stakes of the story should be easy to understand early in the synopsis and build from there. If there are no stakes, there's little reason to keep reading.

FABLE was only fourteen years old when her home, a ship named the *Lark*, sank into the deep, taking her mother with it. The next morning, her father, SAINT, the most powerful trader in The Narrows, left her on the island of Jeval with only a knife and a promise.

In the four years since she watched him sail away, Fable has become a skilled dredger—a freediver who excavates precious gemstones from the reefs by hand to trade for coin—just like her renowned mother. She has spent every waking moment scraping enough copper together to barter for passage off the island, find Saint, and take her mother's place on his crew. And after she finds a new cache of pyre stone on the reef, she's closer than ever.

But when the other dredgers get wind of her growing coin, she is forced to flee Jeval sooner than planned and put her life into the hands of WEST, the young trader from the other side of The Narrows who buys her stones every two weeks.

The crew of his ship, the *Marigold*, doesn't trust Fable, but West agrees to take her across The Narrows in exchange for almost every coin she's saved. It doesn't take long for Fable to learn that this isn't just any ship or just any crew, and the *Marigold* definitely isn't the simple trading operation West pretends it is.

She sees first-hand the brutality of the traders' world when she witnesses a ruthless crime committed by the crew, and she begins to put the truth together. The *Marigold* is a shadow ship, working for her father and saddled under a debt to him the crew will never be able to repay. And Fable isn't the only one who's suspicious. The crew is beginning to wonder if Fable's secrets are the kind that could get them killed. Most dangerous of them all is the truth about who she is—the daughter of the most powerful trader in The Narrows, who also happens to be their boss.

The perilous journey takes her across the waters she hasn't seen since her mother drowned in their depths. The ship barely survives one of the treacherous storms The Narrows is known for, and her father's power and influence, as well as his growing enemies, are everywhere. At the top of that list is a vicious trader named Zola, whose feud with the crew of the *Marigold* has already taken lives. He also keeps conveniently crossing Fable's path, and it's clear that he knows she is more than she seems.

The *Marigold* finally arrives at its destination and Fable finds her father, but it's not the reunion she's spent the last four years dreaming of. When she asks to join his crew as a dredger the way her mother once did, he refuses, breaking her heart and her spirit. She is sent away with only the inheritance that he's saved for her all these years—the location of the sunken *Lark,* with its precious cargo. She also learns the truth about West, who's been secretly looking out for her on her father's order for the past two years. Her only option is to take Saint's advice and make her own way in the treacherous world she was born into.

The feud with Zola escalates when he makes a violent move against West and slashes the sails of the *Marigold*, leaving the ship dead in the water. When Saint won't come to his own shadow ship's aid, Fable sees an opportunity and returns to the crew of the *Marigold* to offer up the only thing she has—her inheritance. She barters for a permanent place on their crew and in exchange, she will pay their debt to her father, allowing them to break out in their own trade. For reasons Fable doesn't understand, West refuses, but he is outvoted by the crew and Fable has finally found a new beginning. And after learning what West has secretly done for her the last two years, she's also found love. West and Fable agree to trust each other, something that breaks all her father's rules for living the dangerous life of a trader.

Fable leads the crew to the *Lark* and then makes a fragile peace with her father. But just before she can set sail to her new life on the *Marigold*, she is kidnapped by Zola and put onto his ship. She is taken far from The Narrows, where she will learn that the past her mother left behind just may be her future.

SYNOPSIS WORKSHEET

Introduce your protagonist, using a bit more detail and context than you did in the pitch. Be sure to include any pertinent information that hints at their core identity, motivations, and desires.

_____

_____

_____

_____

_____

Who else should be introduced in the synopsis? Whittle each introduced character down to a couple of details we need to know. Remember, only include characters who are indispensable to the protagonist's internal or external arc.

_____

_____

_____

_____

_____

What details about your world do you need to include? If you're writing speculative fiction, steer clear of names or terms you've created that require a lot of contextual explanation unless they are necessary.

_____

_____

_____

_____

_____

What is the inciting incident? Identify the moment the story is set into motion, pulling your protagonist into the events that are about to unfold.

From here, you'll begin following your outline, one major plot point at a time. Don't get lost in the weeds or caught up in too many descriptions, and keep your intended word count in mind. Work your way toward the midpoint, then downhill to the finale.

You must give away the ending of the story, even if it's a twist or a big reveal, and be sure to touch on the culmination of the protagonist's character arc as well, which should have been made clear throughout the synopsis.

Remember, this is just a rough draft, so keep it fun. Once you have all the elements you want to include, start revising until you've trimmed your synopsis down to size.

THE QUERY

There is more than one way to publish a book, which can most easily be broken down into two categories: self-publishing and traditional publishing. With self-publishing opportunities on the rise, many writers are exploring that path; they will not need to seek the representation of a literary agent in order to sell their books. But if you're planning to publish traditionally, you'll almost always need an agent.

The process of shopping your work to agents is referred to as "querying." An agent will represent your work by selling it to a publishing house, negotiating contracts, and generally helping to guide your path as an author. You can find an extensive amount of information about this process online, but this section will help you craft the pitch, or query, you'll be sending to agents.

You may have heard this part of the publishing process called "the query trenches," and there's a reason for that. Wading into the waters of querying will test a writer's passion and resolve over and over again, forcing them to find out just what they're made of. We can't make the process any easier for you, but we can reassure you that you're not alone. Even the most successful authors out there were once just a query in an e-mail inbox, so believe us when we say there is light at the end of the tunnel.

There's a lot riding on your query because it's the first impression a literary agent will get of your book. Bore or confuse them, and you might receive a much-dreaded rejection. Intrigue or wow them, and you might get the coveted request for a partial or full manuscript—and then you'll get them reading your story.

A lot of opinions and strategies exist out there when it comes to queries, but we're going to give you our take in a simple three (okay, technically four) paragraph approach that checks the boxes for most agents. Each of these paragraphs has a specific purpose that allows all the pertinent details to make it into the query without weighing it down.

In the query worksheet, you'll take one paragraph at a time until you have all the components ready to fit together. Be sure to make the query your own by letting your individual voice shine through, and don't be afraid to add some flair. Also don't forget to cross-reference your final query with the agent's submission guidelines to be sure you didn't miss any specific requests.

As you move through the worksheet, use the query example on the next page from Isabel's *Together We Burn* as a reference to visualize how your final query might look.

TOGETHER WE BURN

age and Intro of main character!

world setup!

Eighteen-year-old Zarela Zalvidar is a talented flamenco dancer and daughter of the most famous Dragonador in Hispalia, a land inspired by medieval Spain. People travel miles to see her father fight dragons in his arena, which will one day be hers. Zarela wants nothing more than to uphold her family's honor and to do her part in maintaining their prestigious status in the kingdom.

What main character desires.

Inciting incident!

Except disaster strikes during one celebratory show, and in the carnage, Zarela's life changes in an instant. With the Dragon Guild trying to wrest control of her inheritance from her, Zarela has no choice but to train to become a Dragonador. But when the most talented dragon hunter left in the land—the infuriatingly handsome Arturo Díaz de Montserrat—refuses to help, Zarela cannot take no for an answer.

Journey

Secondary character!

As she secretly trains to survive the arena, Zarela discovers a sinister plot at work against her and her family. If she can't pull off the performance of her life and unmask the culprit behind the devastation of everything she holds dear, she will lose her ancestral home, and will achieve what no Zalvidar before her has ever done: the ruination of her family's name and legacy.

Stakes!

TOGETHER WE BURN is a 115,000-word Young Adult Fantasy novel that will appeal to fans of Adrienne Young's *Fable*, Zoraida Córdova's *Incendiary*, and Shelby Mahurin's *Serpent and Dove*. My debut, *Woven in Moonlight*, hit shelves January 7, 2020. I'm also an illustrator and graphic designer. For a further glimpse into my work, please visit isabelibanez.com or my Instagram: @isabelwriter09.

Comps!

Housekeeping!

QUERY WORKSHEET

Paragraph One

Introduce your characters. Set up your world. Share what your protagonist wants more than anything and what stands in their way.

_____

_____

_____

_____

_____

_____

_____

Paragraph Two

Describe the catalyst, or point of no return, for your protagonist, when their world is upended and they must step into their new reality. Hint at the journey your protagonist will go on.

_____

_____

_____

_____

_____

_____

Paragraph Three

Bring in the stakes. What will happen if your lead doesn't complete their journey? What happens if they fail? Make sure the tension is clear.

_____

_____

_____

_____

_____

_____

_____

Paragraph Four

Sometimes referred to as the "tag," this section is your housekeeping information, including the title, word count, genre, and any special information about yourself you need to share. You may also want to include "comps," which is shorthand for existing published books that you consider to be comparable to yours. This section should be brief and to the point.

_____

_____

_____

_____

_____

_____

_____

Now you're going to revise the paragraphs until you have a final draft of each one to take into your query. As a rule of thumb, your query should be five hundred words or less, which is roughly one single-spaced page. Some agents may have different standards on query length, so be sure to check their submission requirements before you send.

Paragraph One

_____

_____

_____

_____

_____

_____

_____

_____

_____

Paragraph Two

_____

_____

_____

_____

_____

_____

_____

_____

Paragraph Three

_____

_____

_____

_____

_____

_____

_____

_____

_____

_____

Paragraph Four

_____

_____

_____

_____

_____

_____

_____

_____

_____

_____

LITERARY AGENTS

You have your book and you have your query. Now you just need literary agents to send them to. Easier said than done, right?

The good news is that agent research is something you can do throughout the process of writing and revising your novel. Not sure where to start? Head to your local bookstore and read the acknowledgments in the back of books you think will share a readership with your story, or from authors you think your work may resemble in some way. Authors often thank their agents in these acknowledgments, and once you have a name, they are just an internet search away.

This is a great starting place, because looking at which writers an agent already represents is a good indicator of what their tastes might be. You can also look up details about specific agents online in multiple databases and public resources. Doing your due diligence will also show the agent that you are knowledgeable about their client list and what they want to represent, which goes a long way.

Experienced writers know that querying every agent under the sun is a mistake. You want to work with reputable professionals with a track record who have references and who have existing relationships with publishing houses. If you're looking at a new agent who is just starting their career, pay attention to what kind of agency they are working with, what their client list looks like, and which books they've recently represented.

The bottom line: be selective when developing your agent list and don't let your desire to be published get in the way of pairing with an agent who is a good match for you and your work.

In the Agent Tracker, you can start to compile agents you'd like to query, their contact information, and their submission guidelines. Pay special attention to any specific requirements they have listed on their websites, such as including a synopsis or sample pages. Once you have a final list, you can track your queries by date sent, date of follow-up, and the agent's response.

Our best advice is to settle in for the long haul and be prepared to practice patience—but also don't waste time banking on the hope that your current manuscript will land you an agent. Start working on your next idea while you wait on responses to queries so that whatever the outcome, you have momentum to take you forward.

AGENT TRACKER

AGENT NAME:

AGENCY:

CLIENTS:

E-MAIL:

SUBMISSION REQUIREMENTS:

QUERY SENT DATE:

FOLLOW-UP DATE:

AGENT RESPONSE:

AGENT NAME:

AGENCY:

CLIENTS:

E-MAIL:

SUBMISSION REQUIREMENTS:

QUERY SENT DATE:

FOLLOW-UP DATE:

AGENT RESPONSE:

AGENT TRACKER

AGENT NAME:

AGENCY:

CLIENTS:

E-MAIL:

SUBMISSION REQUIREMENTS:

QUERY SENT DATE:

FOLLOW-UP DATE:

AGENT RESPONSE:

AGENT NAME:

AGENCY:

CLIENTS:

E-MAIL:

SUBMISSION REQUIREMENTS:

QUERY SENT DATE:

FOLLOW-UP DATE:

AGENT RESPONSE:

AGENT TRACKER

AGENT NAME:

AGENCY:

CLIENTS:

E-MAIL:

SUBMISSION REQUIREMENTS:

QUERY SENT DATE:

FOLLOW-UP DATE:

AGENT RESPONSE:

AGENT NAME:

AGENCY:

CLIENTS:

E-MAIL:

SUBMISSION REQUIREMENTS:

QUERY SENT DATE:

FOLLOW-UP DATE:

AGENT RESPONSE:

AGENT TRACKER

AGENT NAME:

AGENCY:

CLIENTS:

E-MAIL:

SUBMISSION REQUIREMENTS:

QUERY SENT DATE:

FOLLOW-UP DATE:

AGENT RESPONSE:

AGENT NAME:

AGENCY:

CLIENTS:

E-MAIL:

SUBMISSION REQUIREMENTS:

QUERY SENT DATE:

FOLLOW-UP DATE:

AGENT RESPONSE:

AGENT TRACKER

AGENT NAME:

AGENCY:

CLIENTS:

E-MAIL:

SUBMISSION REQUIREMENTS:

QUERY SENT DATE:

FOLLOW-UP DATE:

AGENT RESPONSE:

AGENT NAME:

AGENCY:

CLIENTS:

E-MAIL:

SUBMISSION REQUIREMENTS:

QUERY SENT DATE:

FOLLOW-UP DATE:

AGENT RESPONSE:

AGENT TRACKER

AGENT NAME:

AGENCY:

CLIENTS:

E-MAIL:

SUBMISSION REQUIREMENTS:

QUERY SENT DATE:

FOLLOW-UP DATE:

AGENT RESPONSE:

AGENT NAME:

AGENCY:

CLIENTS:

E-MAIL:

SUBMISSION REQUIREMENTS:

QUERY SENT DATE:

FOLLOW-UP DATE:

AGENT RESPONSE:

AGENT TRACKER

AGENT NAME: _____

AGENCY: _____

CLIENTS: _____
_____

E-MAIL: _____

SUBMISSION REQUIREMENTS: _____
_____

QUERY SENT DATE: _____

FOLLOW-UP DATE: _____

AGENT RESPONSE: _____

AGENT NAME: _____

AGENCY: _____

CLIENTS: _____
_____

E-MAIL: _____

SUBMISSION REQUIREMENTS: _____
_____

QUERY SENT DATE: _____

FOLLOW-UP DATE: _____

AGENT RESPONSE: _____

AGENT TRACKER

AGENT NAME:

AGENCY:

CLIENTS:

E-MAIL:

SUBMISSION REQUIREMENTS:

QUERY SENT DATE:

FOLLOW-UP DATE:

AGENT RESPONSE:

AGENT NAME:

AGENCY:

CLIENTS:

E-MAIL:

SUBMISSION REQUIREMENTS:

QUERY SENT DATE:

FOLLOW-UP DATE:

AGENT RESPONSE:

AGENT TRACKER

AGENT NAME:

AGENCY:

CLIENTS:

E-MAIL:

SUBMISSION REQUIREMENTS:

QUERY SENT DATE:

FOLLOW-UP DATE:

AGENT RESPONSE:

AGENT NAME:

AGENCY:

CLIENTS:

E-MAIL:

SUBMISSION REQUIREMENTS:

QUERY SENT DATE:

FOLLOW-UP DATE:

AGENT RESPONSE:

AGENT TRACKER

AGENT NAME:

AGENCY:

CLIENTS:

E-MAIL:

SUBMISSION REQUIREMENTS:

QUERY SENT DATE:

FOLLOW-UP DATE:

AGENT RESPONSE:

AGENT NAME:

AGENCY:

CLIENTS:

E-MAIL:

SUBMISSION REQUIREMENTS:

QUERY SENT DATE:

FOLLOW-UP DATE:

AGENT RESPONSE:

AGENT TRACKER

AGENT NAME:

AGENCY:

CLIENTS:

E-MAIL:

SUBMISSION REQUIREMENTS:

QUERY SENT DATE:

FOLLOW-UP DATE:

AGENT RESPONSE:

AGENT NAME:

AGENCY:

CLIENTS:

E-MAIL:

SUBMISSION REQUIREMENTS:

QUERY SENT DATE:

FOLLOW-UP DATE:

AGENT RESPONSE:

AGENT TRACKER

AGENT NAME:

AGENCY:

CLIENTS:

E-MAIL:

SUBMISSION REQUIREMENTS:

QUERY SENT DATE:

FOLLOW-UP DATE:

AGENT RESPONSE:

AGENT NAME:

AGENCY:

CLIENTS:

E-MAIL:

SUBMISSION REQUIREMENTS:

QUERY SENT DATE:

FOLLOW-UP DATE:

AGENT RESPONSE:

AGENT TRACKER

AGENT NAME:

AGENCY:

CLIENTS:

E-MAIL:

SUBMISSION REQUIREMENTS:

QUERY SENT DATE:

FOLLOW-UP DATE:

AGENT RESPONSE:

AGENT NAME:

AGENCY:

CLIENTS:

E-MAIL:

SUBMISSION REQUIREMENTS:

QUERY SENT DATE:

FOLLOW-UP DATE:

AGENT RESPONSE:

AGENT TRACKER

AGENT NAME:

AGENCY:

CLIENTS:

E-MAIL:

SUBMISSION REQUIREMENTS:

QUERY SENT DATE:

FOLLOW-UP DATE:

AGENT RESPONSE:

AGENT NAME:

AGENCY:

CLIENTS:

E-MAIL:

SUBMISSION REQUIREMENTS:

QUERY SENT DATE:

FOLLOW-UP DATE:

AGENT RESPONSE:

AGENT TRACKER

AGENT NAME:

AGENCY:

CLIENTS:

E-MAIL:

SUBMISSION REQUIREMENTS:

QUERY SENT DATE:

FOLLOW-UP DATE:

AGENT RESPONSE:

AGENT NAME:

AGENCY:

CLIENTS:

E-MAIL:

SUBMISSION REQUIREMENTS:

QUERY SENT DATE:

FOLLOW-UP DATE:

AGENT RESPONSE:

AGENT TRACKER

AGENT NAME: _____

AGENCY: _____

CLIENTS: _____
_____

E-MAIL: _____

SUBMISSION REQUIREMENTS: _____
_____

QUERY SENT DATE: _____

FOLLOW-UP DATE: _____

AGENT RESPONSE: _____

AGENT NAME: _____

AGENCY: _____

CLIENTS: _____
_____

E-MAIL: _____

SUBMISSION REQUIREMENTS: _____
_____

QUERY SENT DATE: _____

FOLLOW-UP DATE: _____

AGENT RESPONSE: _____

farewell...

If you've made it this far in the workbook, it means you likely have a working or finished draft of the story you set out to write at the beginning of this journey. Congratulations! You've climbed a mountain that many only ever dream of.

Our hope in creating *The Storyteller's Workbook* was to give you the freedom to create authentically, with just enough structure to get you to the finish line. What we hope you take away from this experience is a sense of empowerment and a newfound confidence in your ability to tell stories, with the knowledge that your intuition is something to be trusted.

The road to publishing, no matter which path you take, is difficult and challenging. There's no way around that. And sometimes it can feel endless. Our best advice is to keep creating, no matter what. Keep following the sparks of inspiration when they find you. Don't be afraid to get lost in your imagination. Whatever lies ahead, that's where the magic is.

We can promise you that.

REWARDS

Writing a book is a huge accomplishment that deserves a little something special. If you're the type of writer who needs a carrot, how will you reward yourself for reaching your milestones? You can choose one big reward to cash in when your novel is completely finished, or you can break it up into smaller goodies for each stage of the process. Plan out your rewards any way you like below. You can have a reward for each goal accomplished, one big one for a final draft, or even a special celebration for when you send your first query.

_____

_____

_____

_____

_____

_____

_____

_____

_____

_____

_____